Updated Second Edition

T0372635

Activity Book 4

with Online Resources

British English

Caroline Nixon & Michael Tomlinson

Cambridge University Press
www.cambridge.org/elt

Cambridge Assessment English
www.cambridgeenglish.org

Information on this title: www.cambridge.org/9781316628775

First published 2008
Second edition 2015
Updated Second edition 2017

40 39 38 37 36 35 34 33 32 31 30 29 28 27 26 25 24 23

Printed in Poland by Opolgraf

A catalogue record for this publication is available from the British Library

ISBN 978-1-316-62877-5 Activity Book with Online Resources 4
ISBN 978-1-316-62769-3 Pupil's Book 4
ISBN 978-1-316-62792-1 Teacher's Book 4
ISBN 978-1-316-62899-7 Class Audio CDs 4
ISBN 978-1-316-62946-8 Teacher's Resource Book with Online Audio 4
ISBN 978-1-316-62865-2 Flashcards 4 (pack of 103)
ISBN 978-1-316-62979-6 Interactive DVD with Teacher's Booklet 4 (PAL/NTSC)
ISBN 978-1-316-62802-7 Presentation Plus 4
ISBN 978-1-316-62855-3 Language Portfolio 4
ISBN 978-1-316-62870-6 Posters 4

Additional resources for this publication at www.cambridge.org/kidsbox

Kid's Box

Activity Book 4

Caroline Nixon & Michael Tomlinson

Hello there!

1 Read and circle.

1 Their dog's (dirtier) / cleaner than their cat.
2 Grandpa Star's younger / older than Mr Star.
3 Stella's taller / shorter than Suzy.
4 Aunt May's hair is shorter / longer than Uncle Fred's hair.
5 Mr Star's smaller / bigger than Simon.
6 Grandma Star's happier / sadder than Mrs Star.

2 Complete the sentences.

1 Lily wants to play badminton .
2 Jim wants to go _____ .
3 Vicky and Peter want to _____ .
4 Sally wants to _____ .
5 Daisy wants _____ .
6 Fred and Paul _____ .
7 Charlie _____ .

3 Sort and write the words.

olcd

_____

nhguyr

_____

sthrtiy

_____

lcveer (crossed out)

clever

c	l	e	v	e	r
h					
i					
l					
d					
r					
e					
n					

augnhty

_____

dlou

_____

uqiet

_____

itrde

_____

4 Kid's Box File.

My name's _____
I'm _____ years old. I've got _____
_____ hair and _____ eyes.
There are _____ people in my family.
They are called _____
_____
I like _____ and _____
I don't like _____
My favourite _____ is _____

5

5 Ask your friend. Complete the questionnaire.

1 Do you wake up at six o'clock?   always ☐   sometimes ☐   never ☐

2 Do you have breakfast in the kitchen?   always ☐   sometimes ☐   never ☐

3 Do you have lunch at school?   always ☐   sometimes ☐   never ☐

4 Do you watch TV after school?   always ☐   sometimes ☐   never ☐

5 Do you go to bed at nine o'clock?   always ☐   sometimes ☐   never ☐

6 Do you go to the park at the weekend?   always ☐   sometimes ☐   never ☐

6 Write about your friend.

1 My friend Peter always wakes up at six o'clock.

2 My friend _____ has breakfast _____

3 My _____ has _____

4 My _____ watches _____

5 _____ goes _____

6 _____

7 Read and match.

1 Hello, Jack. How are you?

 c

2 How old are you?

 ☐

3 What's your name?

 ☐

4 Who's that?

 ☐

5 Whose bike is this?

 ☐

6 Whose tractor is that?

 ☐

a It's my aunt's.

b That's my uncle, Paul.

c I'm fine, thanks.

d It's my uncle's.

e I'm ten.

f Mary.

6

8 Look. Write 'before' or 'after'. Match.

1 She gets up __after__ she wakes up. `b`
2 She washes _____ she has breakfast. ☐
3 She gets dressed _____ she washes. ☐
4 She has breakfast _____ she cleans her teeth. ☐
5 She combs her hair _____ she gets her bag. ☐
6 She catches the bus _____ she puts on her shoes. ☐

9 Circle the odd one out.

1	(trousers)	teacher	doctor	dentist	farmer
2	floor	door	window	stairs	bus
3	library	hospital	supermarket	cinema	lorry
4	bear	snake	rock	lion	bat
5	river	lake	sea	blanket	waterfall
6	plant	grass	cook	tree	leaf
7	son	aunt	driver	uncle	daughter
8	sunny	hot	island	windy	cloudy
9	dentist	scarf	hat	sweater	coat
10	longer	quieter	teacher	shorter	bigger

10 Write. Listen, check and say.

CD1

| ~~name~~ bag start play stand farmer straight |
| man father have grey aunt catch take dance |

s<u>a</u>d	r<u>ai</u>n	c<u>ar</u>
-------------------	____name_____	-------------------
-------------------	-------------------	-------------------
-------------------	-------------------	-------------------
-------------------	-------------------	-------------------
-------------------	-------------------	-------------------

11 Change one letter to make new words.

1 A colour.
2 You sleep in this.
3 Not good.
4 This animal sleeps during the day.
5 This animal likes eating fish.
6 We can drive this.
7 We listen with this.
8 When you're hungry you … .
9 You wear this on your head.

red
hat

 Ha! Ha! Ha!

What do you call a fish with no eyes?

JOKE
BOX

fsh.

12 Write the numbers and join the dots.

Start at number **68**. Find another picture with the same thing in it. Look, there's a plant in **68** and there's a plant in **39**. Write number **39** in the box.

68	39										

Now join the dots.

What is the picture? _____

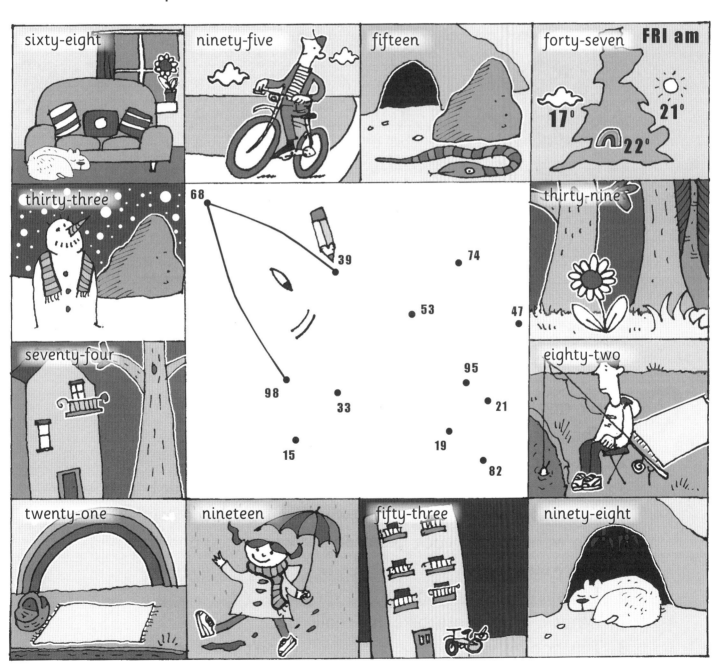

sixty-eight

ninety-five

fifteen

forty-seven **FRI am**
17° 21° 22°

thirty-three

68
39
74
53
47
95
98 33 21
19
15 82

thirty-nine

seventy-four

eighty-two

twenty-one

nineteen

fifty-three

ninety-eight

1 Back to school

1 Find the words.

busy   exciting   boring   careful   difficult   ~~brave~~   slow   quick   terrible

d	z	e	x	s	b	r	a	v	e	a
i	p	h	c	u	f	b	m	e	v	r
f	w	w	a	r	j	i	m	x	c	e
f	z	a	r	p	j	n	f	c	r	k
i	n	l	e	r	e	s	p	i	n	p
c	q	h	f	i	k	l	q	t	p	e
u	u	b	u	s	y	o	h	i	g	u
l	i	j	l	e	i	w	l	n	f	h
t	c	g	b	o	r	i	n	g	d	k
u	k	r	t	e	r	r	i	b	l	e

2 Look at the pictures. Complete the sentences.
1 The man's getting the boy. He's very **b**rave_____ .
2 My aunt thinks television is **b**_____ .
3 My younger sister thinks it's **d**_____ to put her shoes on.
4 You must be **c**_____ when you cross the road.
5 We were at the beach yesterday. It was windy and cold.
   The weather was **t**_____ .
6 The snail is a small animal. It's very **s**_____ .
7 What a great motorbike. It's really **q**_____ !
8 This book is very **e**_____ . I don't want to go to bed.
9 My mum is **b**_____ because she works a lot.

10

3 Complete the questionnaire.

Me

1 I think Music lessons are	boring	☐	easy	☐	exciting	☐
2 I think television is	exciting	☐	terrible	☐	boring	☐
3 I think Maths lessons are	easy	☐	difficult	☐	exciting	☐
4 I think football is	exciting	☐	boring	☐	terrible	☐
5 I think computer games are	terrible	☐	exciting	☐	difficult	☐
6 When I do my homework I am	careful	☐	quick	☐	slow	☐
7 When I go to school I am	quick	☐	slow	☐	careful	☐

4 Ask your friend. Write the answers.

What do you think of computer games?

I think they're exciting.

1 What do you think of computer games? _exciting_
2 What do you think of television? _____
3 What do you think of tennis? _____
4 What do you think of school? _____
5 What do you think of pop music? _____
6 What do you think of comics? _____
7 What do you think of football? _____

5 🔊 **12** CD1 Listen and draw lines. Colour.

Paul   Jane   Mr Edison   Peter   Mary   Jim

6 Read and circle the correct answer.

1 This is the person | when / who / when | teaches children.

2 There | are / is / have | five children in the classroom.

3 Mr Edison's the teacher | what / when / who | is writing on the board.

4 Mary's the girl | where / with / who | is wearing a pink dress.

5 Paul's book is | in / under / on | the desk.

6 Jim's the boy | who / with / why | is sharpening his pencil.

7 Peter's talking | about / to / for | Mary.

8 In the classroom the children | must / can't / mustn't | listen to the teacher

7 **Look at the pictures. Read and correct.**

black beard
1 The man who's painting has got a ~~grey moustache~~.

2 The man who's throwing a ball has got a little white dog.

3 The woman who teaches Music lives in a tall building.

4 The man who's got a moustache rides his horse to school.

5 The woman who likes books gets up at 9 o'clock.

8 **Read and complete the table.**

There are four new teachers at KB Primary School.

Name	Description	Age	Subject	Hobby
		42	English	
Miss Stone				
		28		playing the guitar
	grey curly hair		Music	

1 The woman who teaches Music likes reading. She's 57.
2 The teacher who's called Mr Brown has got a black beard. He is 42.
3 The woman who's 30 has got long fair hair. She teaches Maths.
4 The man who likes playing the guitar has got a brown moustache.
5 The man who likes playing tennis teaches English.
6 The woman who teaches Maths likes horse riding.
7 The man who doesn't teach English teaches Sport. His name's Mr Kelly.
8 The woman who's 57 is called Mrs Bird.

9 🔊 **16** **Write. Listen, check and say.**
CD1

s<u>i</u>t	s<u>ee</u>	f<u>i</u>ve
quick		

easy	smile
~~quick~~	time
night	busy
fly	teach
give	me
think	buy
key	need
finish	

10 **Read and write the words.**

1 She's Stella's friend, but she's older than her.   _Meera_
2 A person who works in a hospital.   _____
3 The opposite of 'always'.   _____
4 A person who looks at teeth every day.   _____
5 There are a lot of these in a forest. Monkeys
   sometimes live in them.   _____
6 The opposite of 'difficult'.   _____
7 This little animal is very slow.   _____

11 **Cross out the words from Activity 10.**

new	~~Meera~~	dentist	likes	doctor	teacher
never	Lenny	snail	trees	his	easy

Use the other words to write a sentence.

_____ _____ _____ _____ _____

Ha! Ha! Ha!

Why is the Maths book sad?

Because it's got a lot of problems.

JOKE BOX

Do you remember?

 _huge_  huge

 ----------------  exciting

 ----------------  brave

 ----------------  careful

 ----------------  difficult

 ----------------   little

 ----------------  slow

 ----------------  quick

----------------  terrible

Can do

I can describe people.

I can describe things.

I can say what I think.

Look and write the number.

1 13.91 m   *Thirteen metres ninety-one centimetres.*
2 20.47 m   _____
3 35.69 m   _____
4 41.54 m   _____
5 78.10 m   _____
6 92.15 m   _____
7 83.12 m   _____
8 64.27 m   _____

Read and answer.

1 Peter is **1.25** m tall. His friend Sam is **19** cm taller than him. How tall is Sam?
   He's one metre forty-four centimetres.

2 Vicky's mum is **9** cm shorter than her dad. Her dad's height is **1.83** m. How tall is Vicky's mum?
   _____

3 The new baby elephant at Park Zoo is **79** cm tall. Its mother is **3.17** m taller than the baby. How tall is the mother?
   _____

4 Fred's garden is **1.62** m longer than Grace's garden. Her garden is **14.11** m long. How long is Fred's garden?
   _____

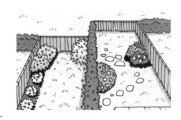

5 Daisy's school is **5.78** m high. Jack's school is **1.13** m higher than Daisy's. How high is Jack's school?
   _____

3 Read the story. Choose a word from the box. Write the correct word next to numbers 1–5. There is one example.

My name is Sally. My dad's a <u>farmer</u> and I live on a big farm in the country. We've got about eighty **(1)** _____ and thirty cows. My dad's always busy and he sometimes works at **(2)** _____! On Saturdays and Sundays, I sometimes help my dad with the animals.

I don't want to be a farmer, I want to be an Art **(3)** _____. I study Art at school, but I only have two lessons a week and I want to **(4)** _____ better pictures.

Every Friday afternoon, after school, my aunt and I catch the bus to the city centre. My aunt goes shopping and I have another longer Art class. It's never **(5)** _____, it's exciting!

boring	sheep	school	night	tiger

teacher	farmer	draw	pretty

(6) Now choose the best name for the story.
Tick one box.

Sally wants to be a farmer ☐

Sally goes shopping with her aunt ☐

Sally wants to be an Art teacher ☐

2 Good sports

1 ▶21 CD1 Listen and draw lines.

Jane

Jim

Mary

Fred

Jack

Daisy

Peter

2 Write the sentences.

tennis	I	difficult.	think	is

1 I_____ think_____ tennis_____ is_____ difficult._____

learn	sail.	to	can	We

2 _____ _____ _____ _____ _____

She's	who	skating.	the girl	likes

3 _____ _____ _____ _____ _____

play	can	You	inside.	basketball

4 _____ _____ _____ _____ _____

you	fishing?	want	Do	to go

5 _____ _____ _____ _____ _____

18

3 Read and complete the table.

Paul, Jim, Sue and Mary are at the Sports Centre. They want to do different things.

Name	Age	Sport	Equipment
			a big ball
		swim	
Sue			
	12		

1 The boy who's twelve wants to climb. He needs strong shoes and a helmet.
2 Mary wants to swim so she needs a towel.
3 Mary and Paul are both twelve.
4 Jim is eleven and Sue is ten.
5 The girl who's ten wants to roller skate. She needs some roller skates and a helmet.
6 The boy who's eleven wants to play volleyball. He needs a big ball.

4 Write the words.

1 What do we call people who teach?   _teachers_
2 What do we call people who dance?   ------------------
3 What do we call people who climb?   ------------------
4 What do we call people who swim?   ------------------
5 What do we call people who ice skate?   ------------------
6 What do we call people who win?   ------------------
7 What do we call people who sing?   ------------------

5 Read and circle the correct answer. Match.

1 She's writing careful /(carefully.)
2 They're running quickly / quick.
3 We're drawing bad / badly.
4 I'm walking slow / slowly.
5 He's reading well / good.
6 You're speaking quietly / quiet.

6 Complete the sentences about you. Use the words in the box.

badly   well   slowly   quickly   carefully   loudly   quietly

1 I sing   _badly_ .
2 I play tennis   _____ .
3 I write   _____ .
4 I read   _____ .
5 I ride my bike   _____ .

6 I eat   _____ .
7 I drink   _____ .
8 I sometimes walk _____ .
9 I play the guitar _____ .
10 I sometimes talk _____ .

7 Now ask a friend.

> Do you sing badly?

> No, I sing really well.

> Do you ... ?

> No, ...

8 Read. Sort and write the words.

1 A place where you can practise football inside.
(ecstrponerts)   _sports centre_
2 A place where you can fish. (ervri)   _____
3 A place where you can go roller skating. (akpr) _____
4 A place where you can sail. (aelk)   _____
5 A place where you can climb trees. (efrsto)   _____
6 A place where you can swim in the sea. (abceh) _____

9 Read and match.

1. We're shouting loudly
2. She's talking quietly
3. He's walking slowly
4. You're running quickly
5. They're winning
6. She's carrying the boxes carefully
7. I need an eraser

a. because your school bus is going.
b. because she doesn't want to drop them.
c. because I'm drawing very badly.
d. because he's got a backache.
e. because she's in the library.
f. because they're playing well.
g. because we're watching an exciting football game.

10 Read and complete the table.

	swim	play football	play the piano	sing	write	climb	draw
Alex							
Meera							
Lenny		well	badly				
Suzy							
Simon							
Stella							

1 The person who plays football well plays the piano badly.
2 The person who swims quickly sings quietly.
3 The person who writes well swims slowly.
4 The person who sings loudly writes slowly.
5 The person who plays the piano well climbs carefully.
6 The person who climbs quickly draws well.

Write. Listen, check and say.

CD1

1 We can see __whales__ in the sea.
2 In _____ we learn about the heart.
3 Vicky's _____ a story about a detective.
4 I always _____ to school.
5 What's the _____ to that question?
6 I want to go to an _____ for my next holiday.
7 The teacher says we _____ talk in the library.
8 I love _____ mountains.
9 John likes _____ to pop music.
10 What's her name? I don't _____ .

island
~~whales~~
know
Science
climbing
walk
mustn't
listening
writing
answer

12 **Complete the crossword.**

What's this sport? _____

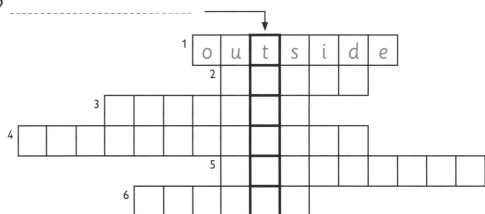

1 The opposite of inside.
2 Hair on a man's face. It's under his mouth.
3 Grandpa Star loves going to the river to catch fish. He loves _____
4 We can play games, run and jump here.
5 The opposite of easy.
6 A person who paints pictures.

Ha! Ha! Ha!

Why can't you play baseball in the afternoon?

Because the bats like to sleep in the day.

JOKE BOX

22

Do you remember?

 *inside*    inside

 _____    outside

 _____    fish

 _____    dance

 _____    sail

 _____    skate

 _____    climb

 _____    run

 _____    skip

 _____    swim

Can do

I can say more action verbs.

I can talk about how I do things.

I can say what I want to do.

batter

1 Order the sentences.

> In baseball the person who throws the ball is called the pitcher. The person who hits the ball is called the batter.

The winning team is the team with more runs at the end of the game. ☐

In baseball there are two teams with nine players each. This is how you play: [1]

Next the batter hits the ball. He or she has to run very quickly. ☐

He or she runs to first base. ☐

First the pitcher throws the ball. ☐

After that he or she runs to third base. ☐

Then he or she runs to second base. ☐

When the batter gets to fourth base he or she gets a 'run'. ☐

pitcher

2 Write about football. Use these words.

football / two teams / eleven players each
first / player from one team / kick ball
players / run / kick / ball
both teams / try / score goals
winning team / more goals / ninety minutes

In football there are _____

_____

_____

_____

_____

Listen and colour and write. There is one example.

Review Units 1 and 2

1 Answer the questions.

1 What's the second letter in [image] ? ___a___

2 What's the third letter in [image] ? _____

3 What's the fourth letter in [image] ? _____

4 What's the first letter in [image] ? _____

5 What's the third letter in [image] ? _____

6 What's the first letter in [image] ? _____

7 What's the second letter in [image] ? _____

8 What's the fourth letter in [image] ? _____

What's the word _____

2 What's wrong with these pictures? Write the answers.

1 _The bat's got a long beard.____

2 _____

3 _____

4 _____

5 _____

6 _____

3 Circle the odd one out.

1	(eight)	first	second	third
2	skip	quick	jump	roller skate
3	well	badly	slowly	tall
4	busy	careful	holiday	terrible
5	earache	Music	Sport	Maths
6	class	teacher	weather	school
7	thirty	first	ninety	forty
8	running	jumping	shopping	swimming
9	family	aunt	uncle	beard
10	skate	famous	difficult	exciting
11	hair	moustache	beard	climb
12	bike	run	swim	hop

4 Now complete the crossword. Write the message.

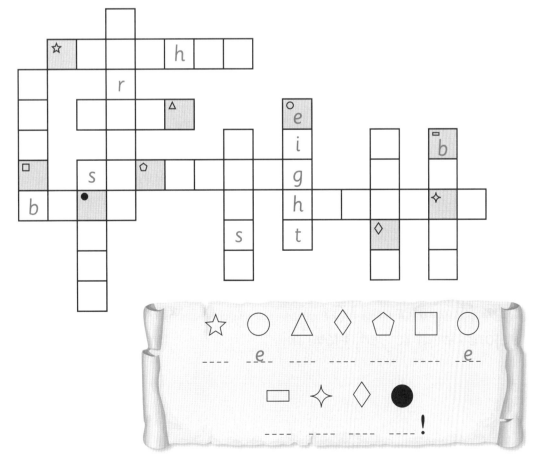

3 Health matters

1 Read Stella's diary.

> ### Friday
> I had a busy day. In the morning I ate a big breakfast and drank a lot of milk. I went to school with Suzy. Before lunch I had my favourite lessons, Maths and Science. I saw my Music teacher and took her my project. It's my new song. After lunch, our English teacher gave us an exam. There were twenty questions. I was the first to finish!

Now look for the past of the verbs.

1 is   was

2 have   _____

3 eat   _____

4 drink   _____

5 go   _____

6 see   _____

7 take   _____

8 give   _____

9 are   _____

2 Complete the diary. Use the past verbs.

> After school I (1) _went_ to the library. There
> (2) _____ a lot of new books about famous people.
> I (3) _____ my Science teacher at the library.
> She (4) _____ me a book on Marie Curie and I
> (5) _____ another book on detectives for Simon.
> He (6) _____ at home in bed because he
> (7) _____ a cold. We (8) _____ fish
> and chips for dinner and I (9) _____ some more
> milk before I went to bed. I love milk!

3 Choose the words.

Last weekend ...

Last weekend was | terrible / great / exciting | . On Saturday morning I | was / wasn't | tired.

There was a good | TV programme / book / breakfast | for me to | eat / read / watch | . In the afternoon

I went to the | shops / park / cinema | with my | friends / mum / dad | . It was | really good / bad / boring | . I took

a | book / camera / dog | with me. After that I was very | hungry / thirsty | but there was

a | café / supermarket | for us to get some | food / drink | . I ate / drank | a burger / some rice / lemonade / some juice | .

It was lovely. I went to bed at | 8 o'clock / 9 o'clock / 10 o'clock | .

4 Now write about your weekend.

Last weekend was

5 Read and complete.

Five children are sitting round a table. We're looking at them from above.

1 The girl sitting between Paul and Jack gave her mum some flowers yesterday. She didn't have lunch at school. She's called Susan.
2 Paul didn't see his friends in the afternoon. He did his homework.
3 Daisy went to a party in the afternoon.

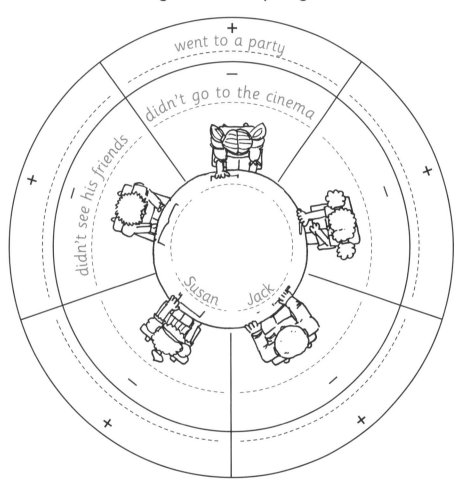

4 The girl who didn't go to a party or give her mum flowers is called Sally. She saw a film at the cinema in the afternoon.
5 The boy who's sitting next to Sally had a stomach-ache, so he didn't eat any food all day.
6 The girl who didn't go to the cinema yesterday is sitting between Paul and Sally.
7 Sally didn't drink any milk at breakfast.

6 Write sentences about the children.

1 *Paul did his homework. He didn't see his friends in the afternoon.*
2 ....
3 ....
4 ....
5 ....

7 Put the words in groups.

> chicken   cousin   burger   teacher   mum
> milk   school   lemonade   hospital   banana
> cinema   juice   park   water   nurse   apple

Places: _____

People: _____

Food: _chicken_____

Drink: _____

8 Use the words from Activity 7 to complete Meera's day.

	go	see	eat	drink
morning	hospital			
afternoon		cousin		
evening				

9 Ask and answer. Complete the table.

Did Meera go to the hospital in the morning?   Yes, she did.

Did she see the nurse?   No, she didn't.

	go	see	eat	drink
morning				
afternoon				
evening				

10 **Write. Listen, check and say.**

CD1

1 Let's go _fishing_ . It's lots of fun!
2 Fred's very fast. He's a good _____ player, too.
3 You must eat lots of fruit and _____ .
4 _____ plays volleyball with her best friend.
5 Ben's a big _____ . He's very tall, too!
6 Basketball's a _____ fast game.
7 Vera visits her grandmother's _____ on Fridays.
8 Bill took a _____ of his father playing baseball.
9 Look at the baby with the big blue _____ !
10 Oh! Look at those _____ flowers!

village
~~fishing~~
football
balloon
vegetables
boy
very
Vicky
beautiful
photo

 11 **Make sentences.**

~~Mary~~	the	to the	the hospital.
Jim didn't	~~had~~	people at	~~cough~~.
Zoe saw	lot of	~~a terrible~~	her medicine?
Did	go	take	doctor.
There were a	Sally	dentist	last week.

1 _Mary had a terrible cough._
2 _____
3 _____
4 _____
5 _____

Ha! Ha! Ha!

Doctor, Doctor, I think I'm a sheep!

That's baaaad.

JOKE BOX

Do you remember?

 Look and read   Say   Fold the page   Write the words   Correct

is	_was_		is	→	was
are			are	→	were
have			have	→	had
go			go	→	went
see			see	→	saw
eat			eat	→	ate
drink			drink	→	drank
give			give	→	gave
take			take	→	took
today	_yesterday_		today		yesterday
this afternoon			this afternoon		yesterday afternoon
tonight			tonight		last night
this week			this week		last week
this year			this year		last year

Can do

I can talk about health matters.

I can talk about the past.

I can ask questions in the past.

Listen and tick. Read and correct.

CD1

 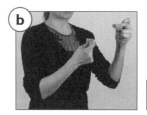 ✓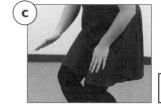

a   b   c

1 She's tapping her face.   No, she isn't. She's clicking her fingers.

  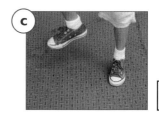

a   b   c

2 He's using his mouth.   _____

a   b   c

3 She's stamping her feet. _____

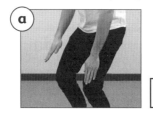 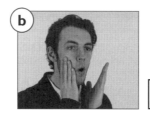 

a   b   c

4 He's hitting his knees.   _____

2 **Read and complete.**

~~body~~   percussion   singing   feet   clap   music   different   instrument

The human (1) _body_ is a great musical (2) _____ and not only for (3) _____ . We can make a lot of (4) _____ sounds. When we (5) _____ our hands, click our fingers or stamp our (6) _____ with rhythm we are making (7) _____ . This kind of music is called body (8) _____ .

3 Listen and write. There is one example.

At the doctor's

When?   _yesterday_____

1   What was the matter?   _____ache

2   Can't eat: _____

3   Where was her aunt on Friday?   _____

4   Her temperature: _____

5   She has to: _____

4 After school club

1 Complete the text. Use the past of the verbs.

Kim and Sally had a great weekend. They went to an activity centre in the countryside with their friend Paul.

On Saturday morning they **(1)** _____started_____ (start) early. First they **(2)** _____ (sail) on the lake. Then, in the afternoon they **(3)** _____ (climb) a mountain. In the evening they **(4)** _____ (cook) burgers outside. The children **(5)** _____ (talk) and **(6)** _____ (laugh) all evening.

On Sunday morning they **(7)** _____ (walk) in the forest. Their teacher **(8)** _____ (plant) a tree and Kim, Sally and Paul **(9)** _____ (help) him.

In the afternoon they **(10)** _____ (play) games. They **(11)** _____ (want) to stop at four o'clock because they **(12)** _____ (need) to go home and sleep!

2 Read and write 'yes' or 'no'.

1 Kim and Sally had a boring weekend. _____no_____
2 On Saturday morning they sailed on the lake. _____
3 In the evening they cooked burgers inside. _____
4 On Sunday afternoon they walked in the forest. _____
5 Their teacher planted a tree. _____
6 In the afternoon they played the piano. _____
7 They stopped at five o'clock. _____

3 Put the words in groups.

like try stop sail play jump drop invite roller skate
close shop cry skip shout dance climb carry hop

+ed	+d	+ped	y+ied
sailed	liked	stopped	tried

4 Write the secret message.

¹ was	² at	³ supermarket	⁴ he	⁵ I	⁶ shouted
⁷ He	⁸ motorbike	⁹ and	¹⁰ laughed	¹¹ Motors	¹² outside
¹³ him	¹⁴ tried	¹⁵ but	¹⁶ jumped	¹⁷ the	¹⁸ Nick
¹⁹ and	²⁰ our	²¹ to	²² pointed	²³ on	²⁴ catch

Lock,
5-14-21-24-18-11. 7-1-12-17-3. 5-22-2-13-9-6-,
15-4-10-9-16-23-20-8!

I tried

Key

5 Match and write.

fifth 5th
.... 3rd
.... 2nd
.... 9th
.... 1st
.... 12th
.... 20th
.... 8th

first   second
eighth   third
              fifth
twentieth   ninth
       twelfth

6 Find the letter. Write three words starting with that letter.

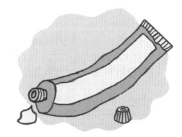

Outside

1 The ninth letter of 'toothpaste'.
   tired, temperature, Thursday

2 The eighth letter of 'baseball'.

Yesterday

3 The fourth letter of 'naughty'.
   ----

4 The tenth letter of 'downstairs'.

5 The sixth letter of 'outside'.

6 The second letter of 'yesterday'.
   ----

7 The fifth letter of 'strong'.

8 The third letter of 'kick'.

Downstairs

7 Read and answer.

It's the first in 'snail', but not in 'mouse'. | s |

It's the second in 'school', but not in 'house'. | ☐ |

It's the third in 'flat' and also in 'stair'. | ☐ |

It's the fourth in 'beard' and also in 'hair'. | ☐ |

It's the fifth in 'careful'. Is it Lock's? | ☐ |

Find the word. It's in Kid's Box! _____

It's the first in 'dog', but not in 'cat'. | ☐ |

It's the second in 'dress', but not in 'hat'. | ☐ |

It's the third in 'green' and also in 'Fred'. | ☐ |

It's the fourth in 'sweater' and also in 'bread'. | ☐ |

It's the fifth in 'swimming pool'. Yes, that's right! | ☐ |

We do this when we sleep at night. _____

8 Read and complete the table.

Name	Position	Activity
Daisy		
	second	
Vicky		ice skated

1 Jim, Daisy, Vicky and Fred were in different competitions last weekend.
2 One danced, one ice skated, one jumped and one played table tennis.
3 Vicky was fourth in her competition and Jim was the boy who came third.
4 Daisy jumped in her competition.
5 Fred was the boy who danced.
6 The girl who came first didn't play table tennis.

9 Write. Listen, check and say.

~~called~~   started   sailed   stopped   kicked   invited
rained   wanted   helped   danced   snowed   decided

'd' – played	't' – walked	'id' – needed
called		

10 Choose the right answers and complete the text.

1	phone	(phoned)	phones	5	climb	climbed	climed
2	us	we	our	6	fifteenth	fifteen	fiveteenth
3	afternoon	two o'clock	Saturday	7	called	cleaned	cooked
4	talk	play	listen	8	waved	watched	washed

To: fred@kidsbox.com   From: simon@kidsbox.com

On Wednesday Alex (1) __phoned__ me. He invited (2) _____
to go to his house on (3) _____ to (4) _____ about the
school show.

We walked to Alex's house with Meera and Lenny. We (5) _____
up to the (6) _____ floor. His mum (7) _____ fish for
lunch. Then we (8) _____ a film on television. It was very funny.

Ha! Ha! Ha!
Why are you sad?
My teacher was angry with me for
something I didn't do.
What was that?

My homework.

JOKE BOX

Do you remember?

1st	first		1st	first
2nd	_____		2nd	second
3rd	_____		3rd	third
4th	_____		4th	fourth
5th	_____		5th	fifth
6th	_____		6th	sixth
7th	_____		7th	seventh
8th	_____		8th	eighth
9th	_____		9th	ninth
10th	_____		10th	tenth
11th	_____		11th	eleventh
12th	_____		12th	twelfth
13th	_____		13th	thirteenth
14th	_____		14th	fourteenth
15th	_____		15th	fifteenth
16th	_____		16th	sixteenth
17th	_____		17th	seventeenth
18th	_____		18th	eighteenth
19th	_____		19th	nineteenth
20th	_____		20th	twentieth

Can do

I can say the numbers 1st to 20th.

I can talk about things I did yesterday.

I can ask questions about last week.

1 Read and think. Write 'play', 'poem' or 'novel'.

1 Actors say the words.	play
2 This can take you two or three weeks to read.	
3 This sometimes has words that rhyme.	
4 This is a long story in a book.	
5 We see this at the theatre.	

2 Choose your poem.

The | bat / snail / frog | and the | giraffe / chicken / lizard | went to the | town / stars / beach

In a beautiful | sea blue hat / leaf green bed / snow white box | .

They took some | jeans / parrots / cheese | , and plenty of | carrots / peas / beans

Covered in | big clean socks / a purple mat / pieces of bread | .

3 Listen and tick (✓) the box. There is one example.

What did Daisy do on Saturday?

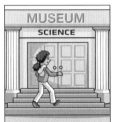  

A ☐ B ✓ C ☐

3 What did Daisy and her friends do first?

A ☐ B ☐ C ☐

1 Who did Daisy go to the park with?

A ☐ B ☐ C ☐

4 What did they have for lunch?

A ☐ B ☐ C ☐

2 What time did they go to the park?

A ☐ B ☐ C ☐

5 How did Daisy and her friends go home?

A ☐ B ☐ C ☐

Review Units  3 and 4

1 Find the past of the verbs.

~~are~~	have	go	take	see
eat	drink	give		wash
try	is	like	fish	skate

s	k	a	t	e	d	w	s	f	l	m
w	w	t	s	g	d	a	y	i	i	h
e	t	w	b	a	d	s	h	s	k	a
n	s	o	r	v	w	a	s	h	e	d
t	h	c	o	e	t	r	i	e	d	n
d	r	a	n	k	g	e	o	d	o	a
e	o	w	e	r	e	p	t	a	t	e

2 Complete the sentences with words from Activity 1.

1 Jim __went__ to the hospital to see his grandmother.

2 Sue _____ a lot of water because she was thirsty.

3 Peter _____ sick last week so he _____ the doctor.

4 Vicky _____ a bad cold so she _____ some medicine last night.

5 Mary and Sally _____ ill yesterday because they _____ a lot of chocolate.

6 Fred _____ his mother some flowers for her birthday.

3 Read and answer. Write 'Yes, I did' or 'No, I didn't'.

1 Did you go to the cinema last Saturday?   _____

2 Did you get up early yesterday?   _____

3 Did you play basketball last week?   _____

4 Did you need a scarf yesterday?   _____

5 Did you dance last weekend?   _____

44

4 Circle the odd one out.

1 headache   (moustache)   earache   backache
2 had   phoned   went   gave
3 between   behind   awake   down
4 quickly   worse   slowly   carefully
5 neck   back   shoulders   kick
6 ate   drank   closed   saw
7 hurt   first   second   eighth
8 cry   carry   sailed   try
9 skip   danced   jump   hop
10 shouted   needed   writes   started
11 thirty   forty   sixty   twentieth
12 tired   pointed   started   shouted

5 Now complete the crossword. Write the message.

45

5 Exploring our world

1 Make sentences.

1	The explorer found	**a)**	photos of polar bears.
2	He caught a lot	**b)**	at five o'clock in the morning.
3	They came	**c)**	camp in the forest.
4	She took some	**d)**	a map, but they got lost.
5	We made a	**e)**	home two months after the start of the expedition
6	They got up	**f)**	of fish in the lake.
7	I lost my	**g)**	sailing in a small boat.
8	You could	**h)**	map so I didn't know where to go.
9	They had	**i)**	a new island.
10	They went	**j)**	drink water from snow when you were thirsty.

2 Make a wordsearch.

Choose seven verbs.
Write them in the past
on the table.
Write the verbs here:

find ....

can ....

....

....

....

....

....

c									
o			f	o	u	n	d		
u									
l									
d									

3 Now look at your friend's wordsearch and find the words.

4 Ask and answer.

Could Vicky swim when she was three?

No, she couldn't.

Could Vicky swim when she was five?

Yes, she could.

5 Ask your friends and tick or cross the boxes.

Could you walk when you were one?

No, I couldn't.

Names	walk (1 year old)	talk (2 years old)	write (4 years old)	swim (5 years old)	read (6 years old)	ride a bike (8 years old)
Me						

6 Match and say.

1 He couldn't find his toothpaste
2 She couldn't find her glasses
3 He couldn't find his coat
4 I couldn't find my camera
5 We couldn't find our books
6 She couldn't find her phone

so

a we didn't do our homework.
b I couldn't take any photos.
c she couldn't talk to her friend.
d he couldn't clean his teeth.
e she couldn't read her book.
f he had to wear a jacket.

7 Read and complete.

What's the opposite of … ?

1 interesting
2 difficult
3 good
4 straight
5 clean
6 wrong
7 last
8 quiet
9 new

	b	o	r	i	n	g

What's the secret word? _____

8 Read and match.

1 Peter's test is more difficult than Vicky's.
2 This film is more exciting than that one.
3 The programme about snails is more boring than the one about sharks.
4 She's more famous than him.
5 She's more careful than him.
6 Her homework is better than his.

9 Make sentences.

thirsty	careful	happy	famous	~~hungry~~	strong	dirty

1 Simon's hungrier than Stella.

2 ....

3 ....

4 ....

5 ....

6 ....

7 ....

10 Compare Tom's days. Choose words from the box.

the weather (good / bad / sunny)   Tom (hungry / happy / tired)
the lesson (exciting / boring / difficult)

Wednesday   Sunday

Tom was hungrier on Wednesday than on Sunday.

Write. Listen, check and say.

1 sh_ir_t	**2** p____son	**3** w____ld	**4** b____ger
5 n____se	**6** sk____t	**7** w____k	**8** l____n

(12) **Match and colour the squares.**

It's mine.

It's their garden.
grey

They're yours.

It's ours.

They're his trees.
pink

They're his.

They're hers.

It's my bike.
green

It's our world.
red

It's theirs.

They're your beaches.
purple

They're her plants.
blue

 Ha! Ha! Ha!

Which side of a polar bear has more hair?

The outside.

JOKE BOX

50

Do you remember?

catch	_caught_	catch	→	caught
find	----------	find	→	found
get	----------	get	→	got
make	----------	make	→	made
can	----------	can	→	could
lose	----------	lose	→	lost
come	----------	come	→	came

careful	_more careful_	careful	more careful
difficult	----------	difficult	more difficult
famous	----------	famous	more famous
good	----------	good	better
exciting	----------	exciting	more exciting
boring	----------	boring	more boring
easy	----------	easy	easier

Can do

I can talk about events in the past.

I can compare people and things.

I can say what's mine and what's yours.

1 Read and match.

1 Polar bears are endangered because …

2 Brown bears are endangered because they're …

3 Some kinds of monkeys are endangered …

4 Whales are endangered …

5 Pandas are endangered because …

a … losing their habitat.

b … because oceans are getting dirtier.

c … it's difficult for them to get food.

d … oceans are getting hotter.

e … because forests are getting smaller.

2 Colour the boxes and put the text in order.

pink	Arctic animals have a smaller habitat	yellow	
green	world changes the ice in the Arctic	brown	
red	bigger fish or sea animals to find	grey 1	
brown	and Antarctic to water. Polar bears and other	pink	
black	live in hotter water so it's difficult for the	red	
orange 1	or walking. What other things can we do to help?	pink	
purple	hotter. Some small fish and sea animals can't	black	
grey 1	food. We can help by using bikes	orange 1	
orange 2	makes our world hotter. A hotter	green	
yellow	because the ice cap is smaller. The	grey 2	
white	Look at what happens when we use cars.	blue	1
grey 2	water in our seas is also	purple	
blue	Cars make the air dirty and dirty air	orange 2	

3 Read the text. Choose the right words and write them on the lines.

Blue Whales

Example | Blue whales are blue or grey and _they_ live in all the

1 | oceans in the world. They _____ very small sea animals,

small fish and plants. Blue whales are bigger than all other animals.

2 | _____ bodies are longer than two buses and they've

3 | _____ very big mouths. About a hundred people can

4 | stand in a blue whale's mouth! On _____ first day of its

5 | life, a baby blue whale is bigger _____ a grown-up hippo.

It drinks about four hundred litres of milk every day and it grows

very quickly.

Example	it	she	they
1	eat	eating	ate
2	Her	His	Their
3	got	get	getting
4	the	a	some
5	then	that	than

6 Technology

1 Sort and write the words.

1	mcrtpoue	_computer_		

2	recens		**5** elima	
3	esumo		**6** oeidv	
4	utobnt		**7** ninttree	
			8 yrMa3Plpe	

2 Read and circle the correct answer.

KBX4 instructions

1 To turn on the computer you push the mouse / screen / button.
2 Then you turn on the screen / video / email.
3 To find your place on the screen you move the computer / MP3 / mouse.
4 You can write an MP3 player / an email / a TV to your friend.
5 You can look for information on the mouse / internet / button.

54

3 **Listen and write. There is one example.**

Shopping

1 Jack went shopping with his mum and ___dad___

2 They bought _____

3 Who is it for? _____

4 He needs it to _____

5 It cost £ _____

4 **Write the sentences in order.**

1 ⟨ weren't ⟩⟨ years ago. ⟩⟨ any ⟩⟨ There ⟩⟨ a hundred ⟩⟨ mobile phones ⟩

There weren't any mobile phones a hundred years ago.

2 (you can) (use it.) (to turn) (You have) (the computer on) (before)

----

3 { to text your friends } { It's easier } { emails. } { than write them }

----

4 (can use) (to text) (You) (your) (a mobile phone) (friends.)

----

5 | listen to | | on our computers. | | We can | | music |

----

6 (are)(than paper books.)(and smaller)(E-books)(better)

----

7 (the internet)(on)(use)(We can)(some mobile phones.)

----

5 Match. Write the words.

One of each is a past verb.

1. bought
   bottle

6. c_____
   c_____

2. ga_____
   ga_____

7. d_____
   d_____

3. w_____
   w_____

8. p_____
   p_____

4. ca_____
   ca_____

9. kn_____
   kn_____

5. th_____
   th_____

10. ch_____
    ch_____

~~ttle~~   reful

ough

rden

eather

inner

aught   icnic

~~ught~~

ent   id

ee

ew

ut

ve

ought   anks   ose

me   ips

6 Tick six words. Play bingo.

BINGO!!! BINGO!!! BINGO!!! BINGO!!! BINGO!!! BINGO!!!

buy ☐	get ☐	have ☐	see ☐
catch ☐	bring ☐	is ☐	say ☐
choose ☐	go ☐	put ☐	take ☐
come ☐	know ☐	read ☐	think ☐

BINGO!!! BINGO!!! BINGO!!! BINGO!!! BINGO!!! BINGO!!!

7 Answer the questions.

1 Mary had forty-seven computer games. She gave her younger brother fifteen and her older brother gave her twelve. How many has she got now?

forty-four _____

2 Farmer Green had eleven lemon trees and twenty orange trees. He bought eight more lemon trees on the internet. How many trees did he have then? _____

3 Grandpa bought a new fishing DVD. Then he went fishing. He caught thirty-two fish, but he dropped eight in the river. How many fish did he take home? _____

4 Peter had twenty-five apps on his mobile phone. He bought nineteen more apps on the internet. He deleted four apps because he didn't like them. How many apps has he got now?

_____

8 Match the questions and answers.

1 What did they give their mother for her birthday?
2 Why did he put on his coat?
3 When did she take these photos?
4 Which floor did they go up to?
5 Who did you see yesterday afternoon?
6 How many fish did Grandpa catch?
7 What time did you get up last Friday?

a They went up to the twelfth floor.
b We got up at eight o'clock.
c They gave her a red scarf.
d Because it was cold outside.
e He caught four.
f I saw my aunt.
g She took them last weekend.

9 🔊 **29** **Match the rhyming words. Listen, check and say.**
CD2

1	sport	..d..	**a)** water	6	door	..i..	**f)** talked
2	Paul	......	**b)** bought	7	smaller	......	**g)** hall
3	daughter	......	**c)** floor	8	walked	......	**h)** thought
4	caught	......	**d)** short	9	call	......	**i)** four
5	more	......	**e)** small	10	taught	......	**j)** taller

10 **Make sentences.**

~~We go~~	loves	cousin	was three.
I couldn't use	~~to the~~	computer for	on the internet.
She	email their	when I	his mum.
He bought	a new	texting	in India.
They wanted to	a laptop	apps	~~every Saturday.~~
You chose	some	~~cinema~~	her friends.

1 We go to the cinema every Saturday.
2
3
4
5
6

Ha! Ha! Ha!

Susan, your homework, 'My computer', is the
same as your brother's. Did you copy his?

No sir, it's the same computer!

JOKE BOX

Do you remember?

bring	_brought_	bring	→	brought
buy	-----------------	buy	→	bought
choose	-----------------	choose	→	chose
read	-----------------	read	→	read
think	-----------------	think	→	thought
put	-----------------	put	→	put
say	-----------------	say	→	said
know	-----------------	know	→	knew

Can do

I can write 'technology' words.			
I can talk about computers and the internet.			
I can say more verbs in the past.			

1 Read and match. Write the sentences.

a

b

c

d
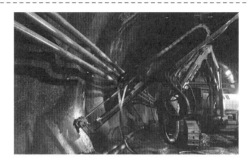

1 Robots can work underground.
2 Robots build things in factories.

3 Robots can help us to explore space.
4 Robots can do jobs in the house for us.

2 Read and correct.

1 A robot is a machine which makes work more difficult for humans.
   A robot is a machine which makes work easier for humans.

2 Robots can't do jobs which are dangerous.

3 Robots can't move around the house.

4 It's easier for robots to dance in factories.

5 Robots can't fix things.

6 Robots are always ill and tired.

Where did Charlie go with these people?
CD2 Listen and write a letter in each box. There is one example.

 Mum H

 Aunt Daisy ☐

 Dad ☐

 Lily ☐

 Grandma ☐

 Fred ☐

Review Units 5 and 6

1 What can you see? Tick the boxes.

moon ☐   orange ☐   river ☐   snail ☐   cage ☐   plant ☐

sweater ☐   blanket ☐   glass ☐   comic ☐   road ☐

cup ✓

beard ☐   bottle ☐

CD ☐

dog ☐   sun ☐

picnic ☐   rock ☐

leaves ☐

parrot ☐   email ☐

moustache ☐   banana ☐

toothbrush ☐   rabbit ☐   grown-up ☐   uncle ☐

2 What can't you see? Write the words.

1 _uncle_   4 _____   7 _____

2 _____   5 _____   8 _____

3 _____   6 _____

3 Find the word. Use the first letters from Activity 2.

☐ ☐ ☐ ☐ u ☐ ☐ ☐

_____

4 Circle the odd one out.

1	bought	thought	brought	(sailed)
2	ticket	button	mouse	screen
3	plant	DVD	MP3	app
4	better	dirtier	quickly	funnier
5	bounced	between	behind	above
6	sharks	bears	whales	dolphins
7	river	cave	sea	ocean
8	drank	swam	liked	gave
9	Wednesday	evening	Sunday	Friday
10	was	were	went	where
11	weather	hotter	colder	quicker
12	came	made	found	know

5 Now complete the crossword. Write the message.

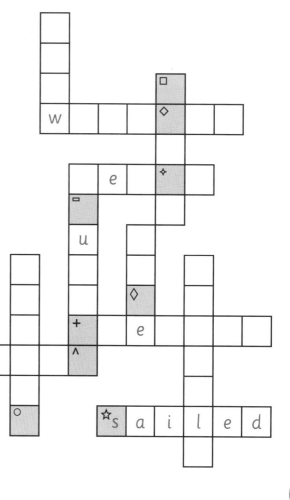

7 At the zoo

1 Make sentences.

The dolphin	lives	in	world.
Penguins	the loudest	sea	the forest.
~~The polar bear~~	can't drink	animal in the	~~on the land~~.
The blue whale is	live	~~meat-eating animal~~	Antarctica.
The parrot	~~is the biggest~~	in	water.

1 *The polar bear is the biggest meat-eating animal on the land.*

2 _____

3 _____

4 _____

5 _____

2 Complete the text about the giraffe family.

| father | mother | sister | brother | grandfather | aunt |

In the giraffe family, _____aunt_____ giraffe is the most beautiful. _____ giraffe is the tallest. _____ giraffe is the youngest and _____ giraffe is the oldest . The cleverest giraffe in the family is _____ giraffe. _____ giraffe is the loudest giraffe in the family.

3 Which animal is it?

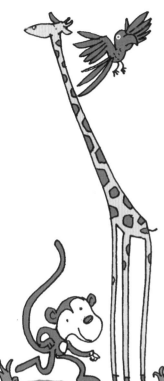

1 This is the tallest animal. It's got four legs and a very long neck.   *giraffe*

2 It's the biggest land animal. It's got two very big ears.   ----------------

3 Some people think this is one of the most beautiful animals. It can fly.   ----------------

4 This is the best animal at climbing trees. It can be very naughty too.   ----------------

5 This is the most dangerous animal. It can also swim.   ----------------

6 This is the quickest animal here. It can also climb trees.   ----------------

4 Ask questions and write the answers.

> Ask four friends about their family.

	1	2	3	4
1 Who's the oldest?				
2 Who's the youngest?				
3 Who's the quietest?				
4 Who's the strongest?				
5 Who's the tallest?				
6 Who's the best at drawing?				
7 Who's the worst at singing?				
8 Who's the loudest?				

5 **37** **CD2** Listen and write the letter.

6 Make a wordsearch.

Choose seven verbs. Write them in the past on the table. Write the verbs here:

drive

fly

_____

_____

_____

_____

_____

	d	r	o	v	e				
	f	l	e	w					

7 Now look at your friend's wordsearch and find the words. Write three sentences with the words.

1 _____

2 _____

3 _____

8 What did the animals do? Sort and write the words.

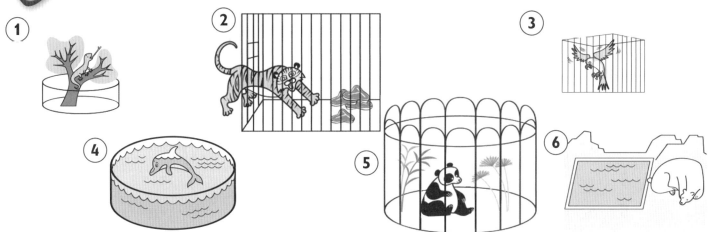

1 The lizard ~~tea~~ _ate_ the fly in the little round cage with a little tree in it.

2 The tiger *nar* _____ into the big square cage. There were lots of big pieces of meat in it.

3 The parrot *lefw* _____ round the small square cage.

4 The dolphin *sawm* _____ quickly round the big round pool.

5 The panda *tsa* _____ in the big round cage. It was very clean.

6 The polar bear *epslt* _____ next to the big square pool.

9 Complete the sentences. Write 'into', 'out of', 'along' or 'round'.

1 The train came _out of_ the station.

2 They flew _____ the bear's head.

3 Peter went _____ the library.

4 Mary came _____ the hospital.

5 The sharks swam _____ the island.

6 The cat walked _____ the wall.

10 🔊 **41** Match the rhyming words. Listen, check and say.
CD2

1 school _d_   **a)** look   6 use   _i_   **f)** blue
2 choose _____   **b)** two   7 foot _____ **g)** book
3 zoo   _____   **c)** could   8 flew _____ **h)** balloon
4 took   _____   **d)** pool   9 moon _____ **i)** lose
5 good   _____   **e)** shoes   10 cook _____ **j)** put

11 Match the questions and answers.

1 Did the kitten sleep in the garden yesterday?   **a** Yes, they do.
2 Could Sally swim with the dolphins?   **b** Yes, they can.
3 Was there a shark at the zoo?   **c** No, it didn't.
4 Do monkeys climb better than bears?   **d** Yes, they could.
5 Can bears swim?   **e** No, there wasn't.
6 Were the elephants the biggest animals at the zoo?   **f** Yes, they were.
7 Did Zoe's dad walk along the beach yesterday?   **g** No, she couldn't.
8 Could the children feed the parrots at the zoo?   **h** Yes, he did.

12 Ask and answer.

What's the past of drive?

Drove.

What's the past of … ?

Ha! Ha! Ha!

JOKE BOX

Where can you see a zebra crossing?

Outside the zoo!

Do you remember?

 Look and read   Say   Fold the page   Write the words   Correct

in ....   in

....   above

....   below

....   in front of

....   behind

....   next to

....   between

....   opposite

....   along

....   out of

....   round

Can do

I can say more verbs in the past.

I can talk about animals at the zoo.

I can talk about the biggest, the best and the tallest things.

1 Match. Write the word.

~~dog~~ horse bat bear whale rabbit

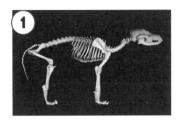
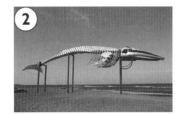
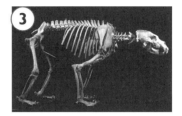

dog _____

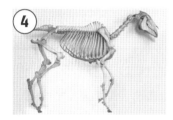
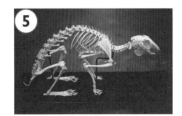

_____

2 Write the sentences in order.

1 [got the] [A giraffe has] [of neck] [same number] [bones as a human.]

A giraffe has got the same number of neck bones as a human.

2 [have got] [and legs.] [Some monkeys] [long arms]

_____

3 [to swim.] [A crocodile's] [helps it] [strong] [tail]

_____

4 [is all an] [together.] [animal's bones] [A skeleton]

_____

5 [Crocodiles] [eyes on the top] [of their heads.] [have got big]

_____

6 [the human] [bone in] [skeleton is] [The longest] [in the leg.]

_____

Read the text and choose the best answer.
Sally is talking to her friend Jack.

Example

Sally: What are you reading, Jack?
Jack: A No, I'm not.
 B A book about animals.
C I'm writing.

Questions

1 Sally: Do you like animals?
  Jack: A I haven't got a dog.
  B No, thanks.
  C I love them.

2 Sally: Which is your favourite animal?
  Jack: A Whales are the ugliest.
  B I really love tigers.
  C I don't like chocolate.

3 Sally: Why do you like them?
  Jack: A I think they're the most beautiful animals.
  B I don't think so.
  C I'd like some chips, please.

4 Sally: Did you go to the zoo last week?
  Jack: A Yes, we went on Friday afternoon.
  B Yes, we do.
  C Yes, every Saturday.

5 Sally: What did you do there?
  Jack: A We see the elephants.
  B We don't see the lions.
  C We saw the kangaroos.

6 Sally: Hmm. Do you want an apple?
  Jack: A Yes, please. I like apples.
  B OK. What colour?
  C Yes, a banana.

8 Let's party!

1 Circle the odd one out.

1 a cup of:	tea	(bananas)	coffee	milk
2 a bag of:	fruit	sweets	potatoes	water
3 a bowl of:	soup	salad	noodles	orange juice
4 a glass of:	lemonade	milk	milkshake	apples
5 a bottle of:	water	pears	sauce	lemonade
6 a box of:	cakes	chocolates	eggs	chicken

2 Sort and write the words.

1 There's a *xob of sgeg*. box of eggs
2 There's a *pcu* of *efcoef*.
3 There's a *lsags* of *limk*.
4 There's a *gba* of *spare*.
5 There's a *tetlob* of *ratwe*.
6 There's a *lwbo* of *iturf*.
7 There's a *xbo* of *aresong*.

8

3 Write sentences.

1 <u>Simon wants Stella to open the window.</u>

2 _____

3 _____

4 _____

5 _____

6 _____

4 🔊 **06** **CD3** Listen, colour and write. There is one example.

5 Choose your party.

Last week was | Jack's / Ann's / Paul and Mary's | ninth / tenth / eleventh | birthday. I went

to | his / her / their | party last | Saturday / Wednesday / Friday |. It was | good / exciting / nice |. We ate

| pasta / sandwiches / pancakes | and drank | fruit juice / lemonade / water |. We | played / saw / sang | a funny | song / film / game |.

I gave | him / her / them | a book / a CD / a football |. I came home at | seven / eight / nine | o'clock.

6 Look at the picture. Write 'yes' or 'no'.

1 The man with the moustache is talking the most quietly.   yes
2 The younger girl is riding the most carefully.
3 The woman wearing glasses is shouting the most loudly.
4 The boys are riding the best.
5 The older girl is riding the most quickly.
6 The man with the beard is riding the most slowly.

7 Read and complete the table.

Vicky had a party yesterday. All the children wore fancy dress. After the party Vicky's mum couldn't find the children. Can you help her?

1 The girl who didn't wear trousers wore a little white hat.
2 The girl who had a black beard wore white trousers.
3 A boy had a big red nose.
4 A girl wore a big black hat.
5 The boy who wore red trousers also wore an orange hat.
6 Vicky wore a white dress.

Name	trousers	dress	hat	nose	beard
Susan					
Peter					
Vicky			little white		

Who was the clown?   ----------------------------------
Who was the pirate?   ----------------------------------
Who was the nurse?   ----------------------------------

8 Find three words from the same group. ↓ → ↘ ↗

1

panda	lion	giraffe
doctor	worst	bought
film star	drove	nurse

2

model	jumped	longest
kicked	tallest	pirate
best	whale	shark

3

dentist	ate	panda
better	drank	fish
monkey	went	clown

4

pirate	had	snake
could	clown	was
bat	parrot	pop star

Write. Listen, check and say.

| eggs | vegetables | sandwich | wanted | terrible | good | computer |
| quickly | flew | basketball | easy | caught | enjoy | came | holiday |

one syllable	two syllables	three syllables
eggs	sandwich	vegetables

  Listen and tick the box.

Ha! Ha! Ha!

JOKE BOX

Which are the strongest days of the week?

Saturday and Sunday, because the others are weekdays.

Do you remember?

 Look and read   Say   Fold the page   Write the words   Correct

 tea _____   tea

 _____   milkshake

 _____   pancakes

 _____   vegetables

 _____   cheese

 _____   salad

 _____   sauce

 _____   noodles

 _____   glass

 _____   cup

_____   bottle

_____   bowl

_____   box

Can do

I can say more food and container words.

I can talk about things I want someone to do.

I can talk about parties.

77

1 Put the words in groups.

chicken   rice   noodles   milk   grapes   fish   bananas   apples   eggs
beans   peas   cake   chocolate   carrots   yoghurt   bread   sweets

carbohydrates	protein	fruit and vegetables	dairy products	fats and sugar
----------	_chicken_	----------	----------	----------
----------	----------	----------	----------	----------
----------	----------	----------		----------
	----------	----------		
		----------		

2 Read and write.

1 Susan's having a baby. She needs lots of protein. What kinds of food does she have to eat?
She has to eat fish, chicken, beans and eggs.

2 Tom's always hungry. He eats chocolate between meals. What different kinds of food can he eat?

----

3 Peter runs every day. He needs lots of energy. What must he eat?

----

4 Vicky's got a cold. She needs some vitamins to make her better. What must she eat?

----

5 Ben's got a problem with his teeth. He needs to make them stronger. What must he eat?

Listen and draw lines. There is one example.

Peter   May   Jack   Kim

Bill   Jane   Paul

Review Units  7 and 8

1 Find the past of the verbs.

~~are~~	find	ride
buy	fly	run
catch	get	say
choose	give	see
come	go	sing
do	have	sit
draw	is	sleep
drink	know	swim
drive	put	take
eat	read	think

w	d	o	f	a	s	r	a	t	o	o	k
a	i	d	l	g	a	v	e	h	i	n	o
s	d	r	e	w	i	d	t	o	m	s	o
b	f	a	w	e	d	r	p	u	a	a	c
g	e	n	i	n	b	o	u	g	h	t	f
c	a	k	e	t	o	v	t	h	a	m	o
a	t	e	r	s	l	e	p	t	d	o	u
u	k	n	e	w	a	t	s	r	a	n	n
g	o	t	s	a	l	c	h	o	s	e	d
h	n	c	a	m	e	a	t	d	a	t	i
t	o	o	w	r	e	a	d	t	n	n	t
w	e	r	e	h	r	o	d	e	g	a	c

2 Read and choose the picture.

Frank can't find his bag. Can you help him? His bag has got two books and a box of pencils in it. He's got two small bottles of water, an orange and his favourite comic. Which one is his?

a   b   c

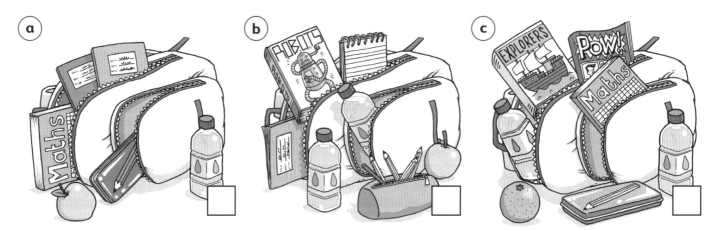

3 Now describe what's in one of the other bags to your friend.

80

Circle the odd one out.

1 tired   thirsty   awake   (badly)

2 carry   climbed   copy   cry

3 twelve   third   eighth   twentieth

4 quickly   well   hungry   slowly

5 tea   coffee   juice   vegetable

6 lift   bottle   cup   glass

7 worse   better   quicker   sweater

8 when   which   were   why

9 soup   ate   pasta   sandwich

10 swam   flew   sat   through

11 dolphin   beard   bat   parrot

12 opposite   into   round   sang

5 Now complete the crossword. Write the message.

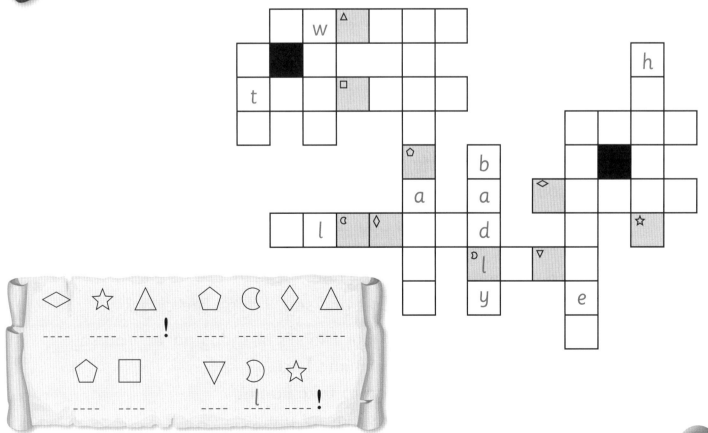

1 **17** CD3 Listen and number.

a

b  `6×6=? /2` **1**

c

d

e  Jack granddad

f

2 Read and choose.

1 When people help you, …
 a) you look at your watch and say, 'Is that the time?'
 b) you smile and say, 'Thank you.'
 c) you say, 'Can I have an apple, please?'

2 After your birthday party …
 a) you say thank you to your parents and help to clean the living room.
 b) you sit on the sofa and watch television.
 c) you have another piece of cake and play with your new toys.

3 In a café, the man gives you your lunch and says, 'Enjoy your food.'
 a) You look at your lunch and start to eat.
 b) You smile and say, 'Thank you.'
 c) You look at your parents and say, 'I don't like cafés.'

4 You're going home after your friend's birthday party. You say,
 a) 'Where's my coat? My mum's here.'
 b) 'Can I have that balloon to take home?'
 c) 'Thanks a lot. That was a great party.'

1 Read and complete.

> Would you like to sit down?   Can you help me, please?
> Shall I carry your shopping?   What's the matter?

2 Read and choose.

1 When Jack sees an old person standing on the bus, he always
   sits down / ~~stands up~~ for them.
2 When Sally sees a younger child with a problem, she always
   helps / takes a photo.
3 When Jim goes to the supermarket with his granddad, he always
   opens / carries the shopping bags.
4 When Vicky plays in the park, she always shares / breaks things with
   the other children.
5 When someone helps Daisy, she always says 'Thank you.' / 'Goodbye.'

1 Look and write. What dangerous things can you see?

1 *The woman is listening to music and running into the road.*

2 --

3 --

4 --

5 --

2 Put the words in order.

1 | It's dangerous | the road. | to roller skate on |

It's dangerous to roller skate on the road.

2 | cross the | You mustn't | cars. | road between |

----

3 | the road at | must cross | You | a zebra crossing. |

----

4 | near busy | You mustn't | roads. | play |

----

5 | your bike. | Wear bright | helmet on | colours and a |

----

1 Read and match.

1 We can make new things from old things.
2 Always put glass bottles in a recycling bin.
3 People make bottles, bowls and glasses from recycled glass.
4 Don't put the wrong things in the recycling bins.
5 Make plastic bottles smaller before you recycle them.
6 When you can't reuse old clothes you can recycle them.

2 Look and write. What good things are the people doing?

1 *The girl is reusing the clothes.*   3 _____

2 _____   4 _____

Grammar reference

★ Read and complete.

1 I think badminton is _ _ _ _ _ _ _ _ _ _ than tennis. (easy)
2 My aunt is _ _ _ _ _ _ _ _ _ _ than my dad. (young)
3 The black cat is _ _ _ _ _ _ _ _ _ _ than the white one. (thin)
4 Simon's hair is _ _ _ _ _ _ _ _ _ _ than Stella's hair. (short)

1 Look and complete.

singing   are   who   's

1 He's the boy who _ _ _ _ _ _ _ _ _ _ reading.
2 They're the girls who _ _ _ _ _ _ _ _ _ _ playing.
3 This is the man _ _ _ _ _ _ _ _ _ _ works at the hospital.
4 She's the woman who's _ _ _ _ _ _ _ _ _ _ .

2 Read and order the words. Make sentences.

dance.   can   You   learn   to

1 _

to   He   learn   to swim.   wants

2 _

to   It's   can   a place   learn   you   sail.   where

3 _

want   They   don't   ice skating   to learn

4 _

3 Look and complete.

did   ate   eat   didn't   Yes

Mum: Did you _ _ _ _ _ _ _ _ _ _ the sweets?
Tom: _ _ _ _ _ _ _ _ _ _ , I did.
Mum: How many _ _ _ _ _ _ _ _ _ _ you have?
Tom: I _ _ _ _ _ _ _ _ _ _ four sweets.
Mum: Did Dad drink the juice?
Tom: No, he _ _ _ _ _ _ _ _ _ _ . I drank the juice too!

4 Read and circle the correct answer.

1 Grandma **danced** / **dancing** yesterday!
2 I **tried** / **trying** to sing the song.
3 She **drop** / **dropped** her books on the floor.
4 We watched the film and **laughs** / **laughed**.

5 Read and circle the correct answer.

1 I read more **slow** / **slowly** than my brother.
2 He writes more **carefully** / **careful** than her.
3 We are **good** / **better** than them at football.
4 The teacher speaks more **loud** / **loudly** than the pupils.

6 Read and complete.

Today was my birthday and my parents (1) _ _ _ _ _ _ _ _ _ _ (buy) me an MP3 player. I (2) _ _ _ _ _ _ _ _ _ _ (put) it in my bag and (3) _ _ _ _ _ _ _ _ _ _ (catch) the bus to school. When I (4) _ _ _ _ _ _ _ _ _ _ (go) into the classroom, I wanted to show my friends but it wasn't in my bag! The teacher (5) _ _ _ _ _ _ _ _ _ _ (say), 'Let's help!' Everyone looked for my present but we couldn't find it. At lunchtime my brother (6) _ _ _ _ _ _ _ _ _ _ (bring) me my MP3 player. I didn't put it in my bag, I put it in his!

7 Match the sentences.

1 Where did you eat lunch?   a) I drew three pictures.
2 Who did they see?   b) I ate it at school.
3 What did you draw?   c) They saw their uncle.

8 Look and complete.

the best   most loudly   worst   most carefully

1 Ben writes the _ _ _ _ _ _ _ _ _ _ _ _ _ _ _ _ _ _ in our class.
2 My drawing is the _ _ _ _ _ _ _ _ _ _ _ _ _ _ _ _ _ . It's terrible!
3 You play your MP3 player the _ _ _ _ _ _ _ _ _ _ _ _ _ _ _ _ _ .
4 She plays badminton _ _ _ _ _ _ _ _ _ _ _ _ _ _ .

Irregular verbs

Infinitive	Past tense
be	was / were
be called	was / were called
bring	brought
buy	bought
can	could
catch	caught
choose	chose
come	came
do	did
draw	drew
drink	drank
drive	drove
dry	dried
eat	ate
fall	fell
find	found
fly	flew
get	got
get (un)dressed	got (un)dressed
get (up / on / off)	got (up / on / off)
give	gave
go	went
go shopping	went shopping
have	had
have (got) to	had (got) to
have got	had got
hide	hid
hit	hit
hold	held
hurt	hurt

Infinitive	Past tense
know	knew
learn	learned / learnt
lose	lost
make	made
mean	meant
must	had to
put	put
put on	put on
read	read
ride	rode
run	ran
say	said
see	saw
sing	sang
sit	sat
sleep	slept
spell	spelled / spelt
stand	stood
swim	swam
take	took
take a photo / picture	took a photo / picture
take off	took off
tell	told
think	thought
throw	threw
understand	understood
wake up	woke up
wear	wore
write	wrote